Original title:
Fern and Fable

Copyright © 2025 Creative Arts Management OÜ
All rights reserved.

Author: Lucas Harrington
ISBN HARDBACK: 978-1-80567-334-7
ISBN PAPERBACK: 978-1-80567-633-1

In the Shade of Green Reveries

In the garden, plants hold court,
A squirrel sneezes, oh what sport!
The daisies giggle in the breeze,
While ants march past with utmost ease.

A gnome with shades, so cool and bright,
Winks at flowers, what a sight!
He whispers tales of where he's been,
To every blade that's tucked in green.

The sun dips low, a soft embrace,
As rabbits hop and try to race.
They tumble, trip, then laugh away,
The funniest show of the entire day.

A ladybug, on roller skates,
Zips around and celebrates.
With every twist, a laugh ensues,
In this wild world of leafy hues.

Ciphers in the Bark

In the woods, where whispers play,
Trees hold secrets, night and day.
Each groove a riddle, each knot a clue,
Squirrels decipher, as they scamper through.

What's that message on the oak?
A joke from nature, or just a poke?
With laughter ringing all around,
The forest chuckles, it's truly profound.

Twilight Reveries in the Leafy Bower

When dusk descends, odd shadows creep,
Crickets whisper, as others sleep.
A rabbit jests with an old wise tree,
'Bet you can't dance as well as me!'

Fireflies blink, a cheeky ballet,
While frogs croon tunes that lead astray.
The night is a stage, under a moonlit dome,
Nature's laughter feels just like home.

The Thicket's Whimsical Narratives

In the thicket where stories sprout,
A fox tells tales, a little loud shout.
'Did you see the hare, in those bright blue socks?
He stole the scene and the farmer's ox!'

Beneath the bramble, the tales unfold,
Of mishaps and antics, all bold and gold.
Yet, in the midst of such wild delight,
A turtle grumbles, 'I just want my night!'

The Scribe of Nature's Palate

With a leafy quill, the forest dude writes,
'Banana peels slip, and beetles have fights.'
Each berry preserves a flavor so sweet,
'Watch out for ants, they dance with their feet!'

In the kitchen of bark, where wonders blend,
Gourmet grub is the latest trend.
But for every pie baked with zest and zeal,
A raccoon might snatch it, oh what a deal!

The Glade's Long-forgotten Romance

In a glade where old trees dance,
Two squirrels planned a sneaky chance.
With acorn hats, they took a stand,
Proposing love at their food stand.

But their plans went a tad awry,
As a cat strolled by with a sly eye.
The dance turned into a mad chase,
No more romance in that sunny place.

Puzzles Lost in the Overgrowth

A rabbit found a jigsaw piece,
Boasted, 'I'll solve it, never cease!'
But with each flap, it lost its way,
Turns out it's just a leaf on display.

With twigs and leaves, the critters gathered,
To help the rabbit with laughter shattered.
They formed a puzzle with silly clues,
And forgot what they came for, all just to snooze.

The Legacy of the Ancient Grove.

In a grove where whispers collide,
The owls plotted a humorous ride.
They wore tiny hats and looked so wise,
While telling tales of silly skies.

With every hoot, the trees did sway,
As laughter echoed, keeping gloom at bay.
They crowned a king from the old bark,
But it turned out, it was just a dark lark!

Whispers of the Green Canopy

Beneath the leaves where shadows loom,
A parrot squawked, causing quite a boom.
It whispered secrets of acorn stew,
Yet forgot the recipe, what a to-do!

The squirrels giggled, their sides were sore,
As the parrot tried to explain some more.
With wings flailing, it missed the point,
And declared the trees their hidden joint!

Dreams Woven in Moss

In the forest, dreams do play,
Mossy beds where squirrels lay.
A rabbit hops, a joke in tow,
Cracking up the tree-line slow.

Toadstools whisper as they grow,
Secret giggles, low and slow.
Dancing shadows in the light,
Making mischief, day and night.

A bear in slippers, oh so clumsy,
Trips on roots, it's rather funny.
The otters sliding down the stream,
With belly laughs and frothy cream.

So come and join this merry band,
With laughter echoing through the land.
In the moss, where dreams expand,
You'll find the humor, nature planned.

The Myth of the Whispering Trees

Trees in whispers, what a tale,
Rustling leaves on a zephyr's sail.
They gossip 'bout the birds in flight,
About the owl that shops at night.

Squirrels boasting, nuts in hand,
Claiming treasures from their land.
Branches stretching, making faces,
Even moss is in on the graces.

A pinecone fell and made a thud,
Causing giggles, sounding like mud.
The trunks are laughing, can't you see?
A comedy show from each old tree.

Legends linger in each ring,
Jokes and stories that they bring.
The woods are filled with laughter free,
A humor shared by all, you see.

Stories Carried on the Breeze

The breeze is filled with tales to tell,
Of runaway goats and an old witch's spell.
Tickling flowers, making them sway,
Spreading giggles along the way.

A dandelion puffs with glee,
Sharing secrets with a bumblebee.
The wind just snickers, lifting leaves,
Turning whispers to playful reprieves.

A paper boat in a puddle floats,
While frogs croak like a band of goats.
Clouds above join in the spree,
Drawing faces on the sky so free.

Every gust, a new surprise,
Brings funny sights before our eyes.
Listen closely, there's joy to seize,
With every story carried on the breeze.

Secrets Beneath the Underbrush

Under leaves, a party brews,
Ladybugs dance in polka shoes.
Mice are hosting, crisps and cheese,
A little snack beneath the trees.

Twirling ferns, a waltz so grand,
Each critter's got a funny plan.
A raccoon juggles acorns bright,
While crickets chirp in sheer delight.

Socks of mushrooms on the ground,
Tripping gnomes, oh what a sound.
A twist, a tumble, oh dear me,
What a sight beneath the tree.

Secrets hum, a bustling fuss,
Life is lively, quite the plus.
Underbrush holds laughter's crush,
In a world where joy can't hush.

Lullabies of the Woodland Realm

In the hush of leafy groves,
The owls croon a sleepy tune.
Squirrels dance on branches wide,
While raccoons play a game of hide.

A fox wears pajamas made of leaves,
And sings to frogs beneath the eaves.
The bunnies hop in rhythm sweet,
Creating a night that's quite a treat.

Legends of the Hidden Glade

In a glade where shadows prance,
Mice hold a tiny dance.
With cheese hats and buttered shoes,
They twirl beneath the silver moon.

A bear in boots struts through the grass,
Declaring that he's top of class.
The badgers cheer, while ants all clap,
For this spectacle, they'll take a nap.

Enchanted Fronds of Memory

Leaves whisper secrets of the past,
While crickets chirp, delighting fast.
A hedgehog juggles acorns bold,
While frogs leap tales that never get old.

The fireflies giggle with tiny lights,
Guiding the way to delightful sights.
Each rustling leaf, a chuckle shared,
In this place where fun is declared.

Chronicles Beneath the Canopy

Under boughs where laughter rings,
A turtle recites the silliest things.
With wiggly worms in a row,
They put on a show that steals the flow.

A chattering crow tells tales of jest,
Of raccoons who failed their treasure quest.
The mushrooms giggle, swaying together,
Dancing along in the light as a feather.

Mossy Tales in Twilight's Breath

In the woods where shadows creep,
Mossy gnomes begin to leap.
They tell jokes in muffled tones,
Tickling roots and old stone bones.

Lichen laughs and toadstools grin,
As fairy tales begin to spin.
With every twist and playful turn,
The night ignites, and lanterns burn.

Echoes of Verdant Stories

A squirrel with a top hat dances,
While chatting plants take silly chances.
Each leaf has a tale to impart,
As grasses sway with playful art.

The whispers lead to giggles loud,
The daisies form a happy crowd.
Together they spin yarns so strange,
While shadows, too, begin to change.

The Curves of Nature's Lore

Wiggly worms in a conga line,
Join the critters, feeling fine!
They twist and turn through soil's embrace,
Cheering on the drumming bass.

Dandelions burst with every cheer,
As bumblebees buzz without fear.
With nature's whims, the night grows bright,
As stories sprout like stars in flight.

Silent Testimonials of the Underbrush

In the quiet of the leafy maze,
Whispers rise in comical ways.
Ants gossip with an acorn's lore,
While mushrooms giggle, yearning for more.

The shadows play cards, all in fun,
While sunbeams peek just to see who's won.
Nature's council, a mix of strange,
In the underbrush where tales arrange.

The Tale of the Twining Vines

In a garden where the whispers play,
Twisted vines dance in a silly way.
They gossip and giggle with leaves so bright,
Chasing bugs that buzz in morning light.

One vine claimed it could reach the moon,
But tripped on a root and sang a tune.
The flowers blushed, they cheered in glee,
As the vine tumbled down like a clumsy bee.

A snail rolled by and laughed so loud,
Sparking a chuckle from a passing cloud.
"Oh, dear vine, your aim's askew!
Stick to the ground, it's safer for you!"

So the laughing vines began to weave,
Their tale of mishaps, too cute to believe.
In the garden where secrets entwine,
Every moment's a jest, oh so divine!

Flowers of Dawn and Deception

At dawn, the flowers posed in a row,
Dressed in colors that steal the show.
But whispers echoed from one to another,
"I think my petals are better than mother!"

The daisies giggled, all plump and neat,
But their stems were wobbly, made for defeat.
"Look at us sway, aren't we chic?"
Oh! What a sight—such a colorful freak!

One flower claimed it could jive and hop,
But flopped on the dance and went down with a plop.
The bees all buzzed, sharing a laugh,
As petals fell down like a comic gaff!

In gardens where tales turn bright and bold,
Flowers boast stories of laughter retold.
Each dawn brings a jest, fresh as a bloom,
Life's comic saga, it brightens the gloom!

Twisted Roots of Atavistic Tales

Down deep where the roots like to creep,
Lurk strange stories that trees love to keep.
A tale of a root with a mind of its own,
Decided to wander, away from home!

"Oh look at me, I'm a trailblazer!"
It shouted to the rocks, feeling quite the razer.
But tangled and twisted in gnarled embrace,
It tripped on a pebble, falling from grace!

Old roots chuckled, their wisdom on display,
"Dear sprout, you need to keep still, I say."
The young root blinked, still feeling spry,
"But fun is my plan, I must surely try!"

So on this journey, the roots told their jokes,
While the branches above cracked wise at the folks.
In the soil's hidden world, laughter prevails,
With twisted roots and their funny tales!

Enigmatic Voices of the Canopy

In the treetops, where secrets bide,
Lived voices that giggled, with nothing to hide.
A parrot squawked in a high-pitched jest,
"Who needs a hat when you've feathers like this?"

The monkeys swung by, making ruckus galore,
"We'd tell you a joke, but we might hit the floor!"
Their laughter echoed through branches so wide,
As leaves danced along with the playful tide.

A wise old owl hooted soft and slow,
"I've seen clever things, but this takes the show!"
As squirrels gathered, their cheeks stuffed with nuts,
"Next time you joke, don't aim at our ruts!"

In this canopied haven, where humor prevails,
Nature crafts stories with giggles and wails.
Amidst the verdant chaos, fun reigns supreme,
Highlighting joy in all nature's gleam!

The Allure of Hidden Canopies

In leafy realms where giggles hide,
Where squirrels plot and robins bide.
They whisper pranks in sunlit glee,
A raucous waltz of leafy spree.

Unseen sprites with nimble feet,
Dancing among the roots so sweet.
Tickling toadstools, lots of cheer,
While crickets croon their nightly beer.

A game of tag in nature's gym,
Where shadows stretch and light grows dim.
Lurking gnomes with grins so wide,
Chasing secrets where wild things slide.

Oh, come and play where mischief reigns,
In verdant halls and hidden lanes.
A merry jive with every twist,
In leafy laughter, none can resist.

Reveries of the Shaded Sanctuary

Beneath the boughs where tales unwind,
A rabbit dons a crown, so blind.
Chasing dreams of royal treats,
With jellybeans and carrot feats.

Old owls wink from crooked trees,
As whispers ride the playful breeze.
In shadows soft, the world's a stage,
Where clowns perform with bated rage.

A jester's hat, a dance of leaves,
Unraveling where no one grieves.
Amusing antics in the glade,
With creatures bold and plans well laid.

So gather 'round the shaded nooks,
Where laughter lives and friendship cooks.
In the sanctuary of pure delight,
Mirth reigns supreme, day and night.

The Song of the Rolling Hills

On rolling hills where laughter treads,
A sneaky goat has swiped our breads.
He winks and grins, a cheeky sight,
While chubby bunnies hop in flight.

The daisies dance, a polka spree,
As clouds conspire, oh such folly.
With breezy tunes, they're on parade,
A merry chorus in sunlit shade.

Sing with me in grassy thickets,
As playful winds toss silly tickets.
Across the vale, joy takes its toll,
With every giggle, we feel whole.

Oh, join the romp, let spirits soar,
In hills that echo laughter's roar.
For every tumble and happy spill,
Creates our song on rolling hill.

Echoes of Forgotten Bloom

In gardens where the misfits dwell,
Petunias plot and lilies yell.
A ruffled rose, with hues so bright,
Mocks the daisy in a silly fight.

Forgotten blooms with tales to tell,
Spin yarns of laughter, they excel.
With petals soft and secrets shared,
They prank the bees who dared not bared.

With whispers low, they swap their hues,
In colors wild, a motley muse.
Oh, let the petals laugh so free,
In echoes of their mystery.

So tread lightly where blooms unite,
For humor thrives in their delight.
Each petal laughs, a fragrant tease,
In gardens rich with joyous breeze.

Midsummer's Fables in Bloom

In a field where daisies talk,
A squirrel learned to dance and walk.
He wore a hat, quite oversized,
And boasted tales of acorns prized.

A rabbit juggled carrots round,
The crowd cheered, laughter was found.
In sunshine bright, they'd hop and skip,
While ants formed bands, a marching trip.

An old wise owl with glasses perched,
Gave wisdom that had all been searched.
He claimed that clouds were just big pies,
And stars were seeds in velvet skies.

With laughter sweet, the day did fade,
In zany dreams, their pranks were laid.
As fireflies lit the evening air,
Their funny fables filled with flair.

Whimsies of the Wildwood

In the woods, a bear wore shorts,
Claiming he had the best of sports.
He raced the hedgehogs, all in glee,
Yet tripped on roots, as you can see.

A fox with flair crafted a cape,
He pranced around, a funny ape.
With shiny rocks and wild ideas,
He staged a play that brought loud cheers.

The raccoons, in a band so fine,
Played tunes that sounded quite divine.
With pots and pans, they had a blast,
Their rhythm wild, they'd dance so fast.

At dusk, the trees began to sway,
With critters laughing, all at play.
Under the moon, they sang with zest,
In wildwood's heart, they found their rest.

The Lyrical Leaves of Lore

Leaves would whisper tales of yore,
About a cat who loved to snore.
His tiny bed, a silver shoe,
A hilarity that always grew.

There danced a sprite with twinkling eyes,
Who turned the mushrooms into pies.
With every nibble, giggles flowed,
In enchanted woods where laughter glowed.

A toadstool band played tunes of cheer,
While crickets chirped, a concert near.
The sun came down, a golden beam,
Illuminating every dream.

As nighttime fell, they all would sing,
Of whimsical tales that joy would bring.
In the rustling leaves, their stories spun,
With laughter bright, they danced as one.

Enchanted Scents of the Wilderness

In meadows where the daisies doubt,
A skunk proclaimed, he loved to shout.
With perfume spritzed, he danced a jig,
While flowers giggled, quite a big.

A porcupine, with quills ablaze,
Told jokes that left them all in haze.
He spun around and tripped, oh dear!
Yet all his pals just cheered in cheer.

With honey bees that played the drums,
They buzzed a beat that surely hums.
A bumble's waltz, a silly sight,
In fragrant fields, they spun with light.

As stars twinkled, they'd share a laugh,
Of runaway mice and silly gaffes.
In wilderness where scents would blend,
Their joyful stories had no end.

The Folklorist's Hideaway

In a nook where stories bloom,
Lies a gnome who sweeps with a broom.
He winks at the elves with mischief bold,
Trading secrets, both new and old.

Wizards in robes, dancing with cheer,
Brew potions that tickle the ear.
A dragon named Fred stops by for tea,
With tales that can make a cat laugh with glee.

The fairies buzz 'round like busy bees,
While trolls pluck the strings of old, broken keys.
It's a ruckus of laughter, a tale turned glee,
Where myths are spun, like yarn from a spree.

So come, take a seat in this laugh-filled glade,
Where even the shadows join in the parade.
Crafts of the past mix with future's delight,
In the hideaway where nonsense takes flight.

The Symphony of the Swaying Glades

In the sway of the trees, a band plays well,
With branches as trumpets and leaves that yell.
The woodpecker drums on an old hollow trunk,
While squirrels in hats do a juggling funk.

A babbling brook sings its own little tune,
As frogs leap along, dressed up like the moon.
Crickets provide the cold-rejected beat,
While raccoons in tuxes tap dance on their feet.

Snakes in bow ties slide by with grace,
Charming the owls with a fast-paced race.
The moon winks down at the merry brigade,
In a concert where every joke is displayed.

So join in the party and wiggle your toes,
Where laughter and music are always in prose.
With a wink and a nod, every creature agrees,
This concert of nonsense is sure to please.

Myths Etched in Green

In the heart of the forest, legends twist tight,
Footprints of giants dance through the night.
Elves plant wild tales in the roots of the trees,
While fish in the streams gossip, far from the breeze.

A troll with a wig swears he's quite divine,
Claiming each mossy stone is really a shrine.
The crow caws laughter, it's hard to ignore,
As he pins the old tales to the forest's door.

Sprites flip pancakes with a magical flick,
Inventing new myths with a sudden quick kick.
Each laugh shakes the leaves, turns whispers to cheer,
In the land of tall tales, there's nothing to fear.

So gather around, let the stories unfold,
With giggles and grins, let the old be retold.
In this green-woven world where the jests intertwine,
You'll find every fable's a source of design.

The Ritual of Renewal and Growth

In springtime's embrace, the critters all scheme,
With birds in their nests, plotting a dream.
A snail in a top hat declares, "Time to sprout!"
While ants throw a party, singing loud, no doubt.

They plant tiny seeds with giggles and glee,
While bees buzz along, sipping sweet honey tea.
The daisies wear crowns made of clover and sun,
Announcing to all that the bloom has begun.

A raccoon on a soapbox declares with flair,
"Let's speak for the gnomes who like spouting hot air!"
Each flower that blossoms brings laughter anew,
As worms in bow ties conga in queues.

So join in the fun, throw your hands in the air,
In this garden of joy, there's laughter to share.
With each little sprout that pops up with mirth,
You'll find in this dance, the true magic of earth.

The Green Tapestry Unfolds

In the garden, whispers weave,
Giggling blooms, so hard to believe.
Daisies dance in silly shoes,
Telling tales, they just can't lose.

A gnome with a rather large hat,
Chases shadows, just like a cat.
He trips on a dandelion spike,
And starts a splat! Oh, what a hike!

Spinning vines like party lights,
The bushes giggle, what a sight!
With every breeze, a chuckle shared,
Nature's jest, we are all ensnared.

So next you stroll past leafy trails,
Listen in for the merry tales.
The world is light, with laughs to bind,
Unraveling joy, if you seek to find.

Shadows in the Leafy Glade

In the glade, shadows play peek-a-boo,
With squirrels sipping tea, how about you?
A raccoon juggles acorns with flair,
While a wise old owl gives them a stare.

The brook sings songs of silly ducks,
Inflatable pinecones, oh what luck!
They waddle past with comical grace,
Trying to keep up in the race.

Amid the trees, a party breaks out,
With frogs on drums, there's no hint of doubt.
They croak and ribbit, leading the band,
In the woods, where fun is well-planned.

So if you wander where shadows dance,
Join the laughter, give life a chance.
The leafy glade, a sight divine,
Where fun thrives more than any wine.

Secrets of the Forest's Heart

Beneath the branches, secrets hide,
With ticklish roots that laugh and glide.
A turtle tells jokes that make you snort,
While a rabbit conducts a wild court.

Buzzing bees with hats so tall,
Dance in circles, round and small.
They share sweet stories, sticky and sweet,
And buzz about the last night's treat.

The trees are eavesdropping, oh so sly,
As a fox puts on a hat, oh my!
He struts and frets with style so grand,
In the heart of a fun-filled land.

Join the chorus where critters unite,
In the forest's heart, the mood is bright.
With laughter echoing near and far,
It's a whimsical place, bizarre and bizarre.

Chronicles of the Untamed

In tales of old, where wild things roam,
A hedgehog dreams of finding a home.
He tries to dance with a skittish hare,
But ends up tangled in brambles and hair.

The fish in the pond give good advice,
Asking frogs to roll dice very nice.
They play games with the warmth of the sun,
Our green world's charm, a tropical fun.

An otter slides down a muddy slope,
Waving at turtles, embracing the hope.
They giggle and splash in this grassy sea,
A fuzzy adventure, so wild and free.

So listen closely, let your heart expand,
In chronicles written by nature's hand.
Where humor blooms in chaotic scenes,
And laughter thrives in all of its means.

Secrets of the Sylvan Dreamscape

In a grove where the mushrooms giggle,
Trees wear hats caught in a wiggle.
Squirrels swap tales of nuts with flair,
While owls practice their stand-up, if you dare.

Breezes whisper secrets of silly sprites,
Chasing their tails on moonlit nights.
They play tricks on the leaves and twigs,
Turning the mundane into comical jigs.

Rabbits wear shoes just to dance,
While foxes plot mischief at a glance.
Oh, how the deer chuckle and snort,
At the antics of this woodland court!

So venture deep where laughter hides,
Amongst the trees where the humor resides.
In this dreamscape of glee and cheer,
You'll find the joy is perfectly clear.

Legends Laced with Verdure

Once a turtle with swagger did share,
He challenged the rabbit to a race, beware!
The hasty hare tripped on his own feet,
While the turtle grinned, oh, what a feat!

In the glades where the snails hold court,
They argue who's fastest but never support.
While the crickets compose an upbeat tune,
As fireflies twirl like stars in June.

Vines twist around, plotting a prank,
Hiding behind a curious plank.
A singing brook mocks the stones in a droll,
While frogs leap around on a slippery stroll.

Legends sprout from leaves and loam,
Where laughter and folly call home.
In these tales woven with green delight,
You'll find mischief from morning to night.

Vignettes from the Sylvan Oasis

In a meadow where daisies wear shades,
The bees buzz around in merry cascades.
Grasshoppers gamble on jumping height,
While the wind makes leaves giggle in flight.

A wise old owl with glasses too grand,
Reads fortunes from footprints in the sand.
While rabbits debate which hat's the best,
Dancing around with style and zest.

The foxes invite everyone to dine,
On mocktails mixed with wildwood wine.
They toast to the trees and the moon above,
Celebrating life with silliness and love!

So stroll through this oasis so bright and fair,
Where laughter is woven in the fresh air.
You'll find that joy is the heart's true quest,
Amidst the antics, nature's jest!

The Ballad of the Hidden Woods

In the hidden woods where the shadows play,
Trees tell stories of the silliest way.
A raccoon swipes snacks with sneaky delight,
While chipmunks argue who's quickest at night.

The brook giggles softly, splashing around,
While frogs croon ballads, a soft croaking sound.
They hold a concert beneath the tall pines,
With fireflies twinkling like musical signs.

A clownish badger juggles with glee,
While beetles dance round like a swarm in spree.
Each critter's a character, silly and bold,
Creating a tale that never gets old.

So wander these woods with some laughter in tow,
Join in the fun, let the joy overflow.
For in this ballad where humor is spun,
You'll find that the hidden woods are quite fun!

Secrets Linger in the Ferny Depths

In the glade where whispers play,
Frogs in tuxedos hop all day.
Squirrels gossip, tails held high,
About the squirrel with the flashy tie.

Mushrooms giggle beneath the shade,
As crickets dance, unafraid.
A secret world where laughter brews,
With every stride and leafy snooze.

The wind tells tales of jumpy bets,
Of mice in capes and strange regrets.
The moon chuckles with a wink,
As shadows frolic—to the brink!

So wander here with silly cheer,
Among the curious fauna near.
For every twist and leafy bend,
Holds laughter's echo—the forest's friend.

The Gossamer Threads of Memory

In webs of dreams where laughter weaves,
A spider spins tales under leaves.
With every thread, a chuckle found,
Recalling pranks from underground.

A ladybug with polka dots,
Reports on spots of silly plots.
The beetles hum their jolly tune,
As squirrels argue—who'll fetch the moon?

Memories float like dandelion fluff,
In a breeze that's never tough.
They gather round for tales to share,
As ants parade without a care.

And if you listen close at night,
The forest laughs in pure delight.
For every moment, bright and wry,
Is spun into a starry sky.

The Arboreal Chronicles of Yore

Once stood trees with stories vast,
Of squirrels and acorns, a comical cast.
In their bark, the laughter rings,
Of forest feasts and funny flings.

Old owls wise, with spectacles on,
Debate the best time to dawn.
With every hoot, a giggle grows,
As leaves roll by in comedic prose.

Rabbits throw a wild tea spree,
Burrowing tales of glee and glee.
While hedgehogs juggle acorns bright,
Creating mayhem under moonlight.

In the shade of every bough,
The chronicles laugh, and take a bow.
For every twist in nature's play,
Bears a story that must stay.

In the Shadow of the Canopies

Underneath the leafy dome,
Lies a world that feels like home.
Where shadows dance and giggles creep,
And fireflies hold a night-time sweep.

A raccoon dons a mask so sly,
Claiming to be a hero shy.
While tree frogs croak their snappy lines,
In harmony with quacking pines.

Late-night meetings of the wise,
Plan how to surprise the owl spies.
With every plot, a chuckle bursts,
In the canopies where laughter thirsts.

So stroll beneath the twinkling glow,
Where nature's jester loves to show.
With every leaf, a tale unfurls,
In shadowed realms, where fun swirls.

Sonnet of the Archetypal Seed

A seed once dreamed of being a tree,
It stretched its arms and said, 'Look at me!'
But winds would giggle and tease it with glee,
'You're just a dot, your future's not free!'

The soil would whisper, 'Oh dear little sprout,
You think you'll be grand? Just wait, hear me out!'
While bugs in the dirt had a dubious pout,
Saying, 'Join the circus, don't wallow in doubt!'

Yet one sunny day, with assistance in sight,
The seed sprouted legs and took off in flight,
'You called me a dot, but look at my height!'
While weeds all around just sighed in their fright.

So, let this be a lesson, short and sweet,
Dream big, dear friends, don't accept defeat!
For even the smallest can dance to the beat,
And who knows, someday, they might just compete!

The Enchanted Thicket's Tale

In a thicket where mischief grew wild,
A rabbit once danced, so gleefully styled,
He tripped on a root, rolling over—oh child!
The trees shook with laughter, they were so beguiled.

A squirrel named Tim, with his bushy old tail,
Declared, 'Folk should dance, or else tell a tale!'
But down came the acorns, it was quite a hail,
Rabbits and squirrels began to turn pale.

'Let's shimmy and shake,' chirped a bold little bird,
'But watch for the rain—it's honestly absurd!'
Yet laughter erupted, more joyful than curbed,
As the thicket held secrets that never deterred.

So if you find woods where the creatures convene,
Join in on the stories, it's a lovely scene!
With magic and giggles, as silly as beans,
Even the shyest shall reign as a queen.

Elegies of the Wildflowers

Oh wildflowers, you bloom in reckless delight,
But bees in a frenzy give quite a fright.
'You think you're so grand,' said a bud full of spite,
'Flailing around like you're ready to fight!'

The daisies then murmured, 'Shhhh, keep it down!'
While poppies were posing, all wearing a crown.
They giggled and winked, with petals their gown,
Saying, 'Watch out for bugs—honey's not brown!'

Amidst all the chatter, a tulip took flight,
'Can you believe flowers, historically slight,
Are now rulers of gardens, oh, what a sight!'
Then they all took a bow, in pure giddy delight.

So here's to the blooms, they'll dance and they'll sway,
Embrace all the laughter that brightens the day!
For petals have stories in every array,
With giggles that linger, come join the bouquet!

Passages through Mossy Realms

In realms where the moss hugs the ground oh so tight,
Lived creatures who plotted from morning till night.
A gnome with a hat, declaring with fright,
'If I don't find my snacks, I won't sleep till light!'

A fox with a grin, oh what mischief unfolded,
Took gnome's tiny cheese, then merrily scolded,
'You snooze, you will lose!' as laughter exploded,
While the mushrooms around them giggled and molded.

Through shadows they dart, this playful grand chase,
The gnome chased the fox, a wild, hasty race.
Yet soon they both fell, in a sunny embrace,
Laughing so hard, they forgot their own place.

So wander this moss with a heart full of jest,
For when you engage with giggles, you're blessed.
The realm's every nook knows laughter, the best,
Join in with the critters, take off on this quest!

Lullabies of the Flora

In the garden, bees do hum,
A sleepy song, oh what a fun!
The daisies dance in soft sunlight,
Tickling leaves, oh what a sight!

Worms wear hats, quite miffed and proud,
While frogs croak songs that draw a crowd.
Each petal flips with silly grace,
Nature's giggles fill the space!

Sunlit beetles in a parade,
Show off their moves, the twirl and fade.
Grasshoppers leap with style so bright,
Inviting all to join the light!

So close your eyes, let dreams unfold,
In this world where laughter's gold.
The flora sings its sweet refrain,
In sleepy tones that spark the brain!

Fables in the Foliage

In a thicket, tales are spun,
Where acorns play, and squirrels run.
The oak tree laughs, its branches sway,
As critters act in their own play.

A clever crow steals a shiny thing,
Dancing in mischief, what joy it brings!
While daisies chatter with dainty flair,
Debating loudly who's the fairest there.

Ladybugs don their polka-dot gear,
While tree frogs croak without any fear.
Each leaf whispers secrets so sly,
In stories told 'neath the vast blue sky.

So gather round, lend an ear,
To nature's fables, filled with cheer.
In every rustle, there's laughter's sound,
Where silly antics truly abound!

The Allure of Unraveled Paths

Winding trails stretch far and wide,
Leading to mischief, arms open wide.
Where flowers giggle at silly ants,
While wind gives leaves their merry chants.

A pathway lined with mushrooms bright,
Where pixies play from day to night.
Each stone holds tales of twists and churns,
In every turn, a lesson to learn.

Rabbits hop with a playful glee,
Drawing maps, as they scamper free.
The sun peeks through, casting a grin,
On paths of wonder, let fun begin!

So take a step, and let it flow,
In this vastness, the laughter grows.
Wander the roads that tickle your feet,
And find the joy in paths so sweet!

Chronicles of the Verdant Veil

Behind the leaves, a tale unfolds,
Of cheeky chaps and daring scolds.
A spider spun a web so grand,
Inviting flies to join the band.

The woodpecker laughed with a rhythmic tap,
While hedgehogs dreamed in a cozy nap.
Squirrels chattered in high delight,
Over walnuts tossed in a playful fight.

Each fable tells of critters bold,
In a world where laughter's worth its gold.
With every rustle, a chuckle's passed,
Nature's comedy forever cast.

So listen close, to stories spun,
In foliage where the laughter's fun.
The chronicles of green and bright,
Bring joy to heart and tickles to sight!

Storytime in the Thicket

In the woods where giggles grow,
Squirrels trade tales, don't you know?
A rabbit's hat, just for a jest,
And hedgehogs dance in silly vests.

The owl reads books upside-down,
While raccoons in tuxedos frown.
A frog with dreams of being grand,
Attempted ballet on lily land.

Mice recite verses, sweet and small,
As fireflies light up the hall.
With each laugh, the night draws near,
A festival of cheer, my dear!

So grab your cap, come join the show,
In this thicket, joy will flow.
The stories here tiptoe and sway,
Funny whispers paint the day.

Enigma of the Wooded Trails

In shadows deep, the paths perplex,
A fox misplaced his new complex.
With maps of cheese for guidance sought,
He found himself in a pickle lot.

The deer, with antlers made of light,
Complains of branches, oh what a plight!
A bear in stripes, quite the charade,
Sells ice cream cones in the glade.

The laughter echoes, round and round,
As mushrooms sway beneath the ground.
Whispers of secrets, soft and loud,
In this puzzle, oh how we're proud!

So take a step down these quirky lanes,
And lose your way with joyous pains.
In the woods, the absurd prevails,
And each adventure tops the tales.

The Language of the Wild

The whispers in the trees do speak,
In giggles high and voices meek.
A chattering chipmunk winds the tale,
Of caffeinated bugs and a mischievous snail.

A parrot in stripes, quite the scholar,
Claims it teaches squirrels to holler.
With each squawk, a jest unfolds,
In the chatter of fur and feathers bold.

On a branch, the cat does muse,
Of dreams involving colorful shoes.
The crickets beat a drum so loud,
To cheer the antics of the crowd.

In nature's tongue, they share their glee,
In every rustle, you might just see.
Join the wild, demand a peek,
For laughter there is never weak!

Epics Cradled in Roots

In the heart of the soil, tales reside,
Of roots that twist and gnarled sides.
A worm becomes a wise old sage,
Spinning legends from a golden page.

The rabbit claims to win the race,
With shoes made of leaves, a hasty pace.
The turtles laugh, "We've heard it all!"
As they sip tea, far from the brawl.

The bushes gossip, oh so sly,
Of a crow who once learned to fly.
But tripped on a branch, what a blunder,
Now it caws in fits of thunder!

Around the roots, the stories nest,
Each one weaves a funny quest.
So gather near, let humor bloom,
With every fable, joy will loom.

Panoply of Petals and Parables

In a garden bright and fair,
A squirrel danced without a care,
He stole a hat from a sleeping cat,
And wore it proudly, imagine that!

The roses giggled with delight,
As daisies twirled, oh what a sight!
The bees buzzed low, in suits of black,
While butterflies joined in a wild hack!

A snail in armor, oh so slick,
Challenged a frog to a racing trick,
With humor brewing in the air,
Nature's jesters formed a quirky square!

The sun beamed down, a jolly host,
As wise old owls baked a toast,
For every petal and each cheer,
A tale was spun, year after year!

Nature's Untold Chronicles

A turtle told a squirrel bold,
Of secrets in the leaves of gold,
"Don't mention me, I'm quite the shy,
But here's a wink, give it a try!"

In shadows deep, the grasses sighed,
As rabbits giggled and bunnies cried,
They played hide and seek near the pond,
While frogs croaked tales of magic beyond!

The trees whispered with a playful grin,
As the wind twirled happily, a little spin,
"Beware the gnome with the crooked nose,
He hoards the fun like a weary prose!"

When night drew near, the moonlit crew,
Danced with stars, just for a few,
With laughter echoing through the glade,
These fables spun, never to fade!

The Enchanted Grove's Embrace

In an enchanted grove so lush,
A raccoon wore a golden brush,
He painted flowers, what a spree,
While chipmunks watched, oh glee, oh glee!

The brook babbled with a cheeky tone,
As frogs debated the best ice cream cone,
One claimed mint, the other strawberry,
While a deer chuckled, feeling merry!

Crickets held a concert at dusk,
To serenade the trees with husk,
But one lost a shoe and jumped amiss,
Making the audience shout in bliss!

As night fell soft with twinkling bright,
Fireflies danced, spreading pure delight,
The grove was alive, laughter ablaze,
In this world of whimsy, all was a craze!

Fables Written in Dewdrops

Each dewdrop sparkled with a tale,
Of how the mouse once set a sail,
To find a cheese that glowed like gold,
With mischief brewing, bold and cold!

A ladybug, in a polka-dot dress,
Told stories of her silly mess,
How she lost her way to the rose,
And crashed with a laugh, heavens knows!

A whispering wind shared gossip low,
Of a snail who dreamed he could fly slow,
"With wings of cheese, I'd zoom the sky!"
He poured out dreams with a hopeful sigh!

As dawn broke with a gentle smile,
The garden bloomed, each petal a mile,
In laughter, all the creatures would leap,
Woven fables, in sunshine deep!

Whispers of the Sylvan Grove

In a glen where shadows play,
A squirrel danced, hip-hip-hooray!
Mushrooms giggled, tickled by sun,
As butterflies plotted their next fun run.

A rabbit wore a sunhat bright,
Claimed it helped him see the light.
While crickets chirped, holding a quiz,
The owl snored loudly, a lazy whiz.

Tree trunks whispered, tales of yore,
As acorns planned a mighty score.
Chasing breezes, the leaves did sway,
In the woodland ball, they'd dance away.

And if you listen close tonight,
You might catch laughter taking flight.
Nature's mischief, oh what a show,
In the grove where the giggles grow.

Tales from the Verdant Canopy

Up high in the branches, a rumor flies,
A flock of owls wear silly ties.
The woodpecker bangs like a drummer's beat,
Claiming he's bringing the forest's heat.

A raccoon with glasses tried to read,
Deciphering maps of a treasure seed.
Silly geese quacked, forming a band,
Steering the turtles with a brave hand.

Branches swayed with an absent-minded breeze,
As the squirrels debated the best of cheese.
Down below, the rabbits played cards,
Betting their fluff in their backyard yards.

The laughter echoed, lively and bright,
Filling the forest with pure delight.
In a canvas of green where stories unfurl,
Every critter has a laugh-filled whirl.

Echoes of the Woodland Lore

Among the ferns, a critter pranced,
A wise old owl, who loved to dance.
With feet so tiny, he'd twirl and spin,
While squirrels in hats cheered him to win.

A hedgehog tried to climb a tree,
But rolled back down, oh woe is he!
The fox brought pies for a snack parade,
While singing songs of the fun they'd made.

In the twilight, shadows grew long,
As the frogs croaked their evening song.
The moon peeked out, a grin so bright,
Saying, "Join the revels, what a sight!"

With every giggle and chortle shared,
The woodland wonders, none unprepared.
In echoes of laughter, life did soar,
A symphony of fun, forever more.

Sprouts of Enchantment

In a garden where magic likes to sneak,
A gnome juggled apples, quite the unique.
While ladybugs danced to a tune so sweet,
And caterpillars boasted their gelato feat.

The daisies whispered funny advice,
"To plant your dreams takes just one slice!"
Crickets debated, who could sing best,
While a shy snail held a singing contest.

Under moonlight, a firefly parade,
Flashing its lights, like a disco cascade.
The hedgehogs rolled up, ready to cheer,
For a night full of wonders and joyous beer.

With seeds of laughter in every nook,
The garden buzzed like a storybook.
With every sprout, enchantment would bloom,
In their cozy corner of merry gloom.

The Sprig's Subtle Song

In the glen where whispers play,
A sprig sings songs of a bright bouquet.
It dances lightly on the breeze,
Tickling noses like a tease.

It tells of squirrels and acorn dreams,
Of funny fables in moonlit beams.
A critter sports a tiny crown,
Declaring all of nature's renown.

The pebbles giggle as they roll,
Under the weight of a chubby mole.
And with each giggle, the flowers sway,
As the sprig sings on through the day.

So join the revel in this light,
Where laughter blooms and spirits bright.
For every sprout has tales untold,
In the woodland, young and old.

Legends of the Burgeoning Bough

Up high on branches bold and green,
Legends lofted, a sight unseen.
An owl in glasses reads a book,
While muddy paws plot in their nook.

The tales of nuts that roll and slip,
And frogs who claim the leadership.
In whispered tones, the breezes share,
The genius blooms of fauna rare.

A butterfly, with tales to tell,
Drinks dew from leaves, oh what a swell!
As bees in chorus hum a tune,
In sunlight's grin and evening's swoon.

So gather round, dear friends so dear,
And lend a smile, erase all fear.
The boughs are busy, don't you see?
Creating silly glee in spree!

The Grove's Eldritch Memory

In the grove where shadows dance,
Eldritch memories take a chance.
A raccoon juggles berries bright,
Creating quite a funny sight.

The trees hold secrets, strange and bold,
As squirrels act like they're controlled.
With prancing steps and winks so sly,
They plot their mischief from on high.

And in this realm, a laughing brook,
Reflects the tales of every nook.
With splashes loud, and bubbles cheer,
Encouraging giggles, never fear.

So prance along the leafy lanes,
Where humor grows, and joy remains.
For in this grove, each twist and turn,
Unfolds a jest, for all to learn.

Folklore of the Ancient Roots

Deep beneath, where whispers twine,
The ancient roots tell tales divine.
With chuckles low and sighs so grand,
They share their lore across the land.

A snail joins in with a hefty claim,
That he can win the fastest game.
While toads croak out their gassy tunes,
And join the laughter 'neath the moons.

The earthworms gossip with wiggles tight,
About the critters that take flight.
A riddle shared, a pun gets passed,
In roots and laughter, friendships cast.

So come and sit upon the ground,
Where roots entwine and joys abound.
For every chuckle, every jest,
Is folklore's treasure, simply blessed.

The Harmonies Beneath the Bark

In a grove where the squirrels joke,
The trees giggle with each gentle poke.
A raccoon strums a twig like a lute,
While branches sway in a leafy suit.

The much-acclaimed snail sings a line,
Unrushed and smooth, oh so divine.
His chorus echoes through the green,
A whimsical tune unlike any seen.

Beneath the bark, a party brews,
With fireflies dancing, lighting cues.
The mushrooms sway in shades of glee,
Their caps adorned, a sight to see.

So if you hear that melodic sound,
Join the revels where joy is found.
In the laughter of leaves we can tell,
Nature's orchestra plays oh so well.

An Anthology of Wild Whispers

In the thicket, secrets float,
The fox recites a funny quote.
The owls giggle, heed the call,
While wise old trees recount it all.

A chipmunk pens a tale so bright,
He jots it down by soft moonlight.
His memoirs filled with daring deeds,
In between munching on his seeds.

The winds play tricks, like pranks of yore,
Stealing hats and running out the door.
With whispers soft, they share their cheer,
Creating chuckles for all to hear.

So gather round, let stories blend,
In a world where laughter has no end.
For every leaf that flutters free,
Is a chapter from the wild we see.

Flickers of Life in Wandering Woods

The sun peeks through, the shadows dance,
While mushrooms wear their finest pants.
A bunny hops with comical grace,
As he plays hide and seek in the space.

The twirling ferns become the show,
With a rabbit judge, oh what a glow!
Each leaf declares a stylish flair,
As creatures prance without a care.

In the wandering woods, a jest is born,
With acorns falling, the laughter's worn.
The laughter swells, a bubbling brook,
Where even the grumpy old toad took a look.

So join the antics where fun ignites,
In the flickers of life, pure delights.
With nature's quirk, let spirits soar,
In this comical world, we want more!

The Spirited Dance of Dew-kissed Leaves

The morning dew begins to twirl,
As each leaf laughs and gives a whirl.
The sun shines bright on shimmering green,
Where nature's giggles can be seen.

With ants forming their merry band,
And crickets chirping, they take a stand.
A ladybug leads the grand parade,
In this leafy disco, the mood is made.

The breezes tease with ticklish tones,
While dandelion seeds play with moans.
Every swirl and twist makes hearts rewind,
In this spirited dance, true joy we find.

So let your cares float in the breeze,
Join the leaves as they sway with ease.
With every giggle that's born today,
The dance of nature will lead the way.

The Dappled Sunlight Chronicles

In beams of bright and dappled light,
A squirrel forgot his acorn tight.
He danced around on branches high,
With laughter echoing through the sky.

The shadows played a silly game,
As flowers whispered secrets, tame.
A bumblebee honked like a clown,
While daisies giggled, oh so brown!

A butterfly fell, quite out of style,
It tripped on petals, made us smile.
A wind gust teased the leaves to sway,
Nature's circus on bright display!

With joy we watch this leafy spree,
The forest chuckles, oh so free.
Each sunbeam sparkles humor bright,
In this woodland of pure delight.

Poems of the Wandering Sapling

A little sprout with dreams so grand,
Hopes to travel, see the land.
But oh! It found that roots hold tight,
And laughed at plans of taking flight.

It asked the wind for some advice,
"Please lift me up! I'll be so nice!"
But gusty breezes only swirled,
The sapling spun in leafy whirls.

A patch of moss, it did proclaim,
"Let's start a comedy! What a game!"
They chuckled low, till the sun arose,
And then the sprout feigned a nose.

So here it stays, a merry tease,
Finding joy in playful breeze.
With every inch, it grows and plays,
In this humorous, green ballet.

The Decorous Dance of the Orchards

In orchards ripe, a party blooms,
Apples sway to merry tunes.
A pear in a tutu twirled around,
While cherries giggled, bouncing sound.

A scarecrow jived with great finesse,
His straw arms flailed in pure excess.
"You're dancing like a wobbly goat!"
The pumpkins yelled, with glee they gloat.

With every jig, the branches creaked,
As waving leaves shared secrets leaked.
The bashful plums began to sway,
Enchanted by this fruity display.

So if you pass the orchard trail,
Don't miss the dance, it won't be stale!
Embrace the joy, let laughter soar,
In nature's gala, there's always more!

The Ancient Grove's Lament

The wise old trees with wrinkled bark,
Tell tales of cheer, in sunlight's spark.
But with a sigh, they share their lore,
Of squirrels stealing nuts galore.

A raven perched on high, he cawed,
"Why's the moss so thick? I'm awed!"
While mushrooms chuckled, sprouting there,
In neon colors—oh, what flair!

The bees were buzzing quite a tune,
They swore they'd dance beneath the moon.
Yet roots complained of hidden stones,
And that ticklish grass of prickly tones.

They laughed through tears of ancient age,
As laughter served as a sturdy page.
In every rustle, every sigh,
The grove finds humor, 'neath the sky.

Tales Woven in Leaf Shadows

In the shade where laughter lies,
A squirrel stole the baker's pies.
With acorns tossed like tiny balls,
He danced beneath the leafy halls.

A rabbit wearing polka dots,
Held court while sipping steaming pots.
The forest critters all agreed,
This woodland life is quite the deed!

A wise old owl perched up high,
Said jokes about the passersby.
"Why did the chicken cross the path?
To dodge the rabbit's funny wrath!"

Each sunrise brings new tales to tell,
With giggles echoing through the dell.
So gather 'round and catch a cheer,
In leaf shadows, fun lives here!

Secrets Beneath the Forest Floor

Beneath the roots where secrets creep,
A mole is telling tales in sleep.
He dreams of cheese and buttered bread,
While ants parade above his head.

Each acorn holds a jest or two,
A story shared by the forest crew.
"Why is the mushroom popping by?
Because he heard the fox say 'hi'!"

Underneath the ground so cool,
The worms are making quite a school.
They wriggle and they twist with glee,
Teaching dance moves, oh so free!

So dive below where laughter roams,
In secret tunnels, they call home.
The world above can miss the score,
Of mirth and joy from the forest floor.

The Myth of the Whispering Grove

In the grove, where whispers play,
The trees tell jokes at the end of day.
A gnarled oak with knobby knees,
Cracks puns that tickle with the breeze.

A chipmunk took up stand-up right,
Using shadows for his spotlight.
"Why don't trees just ever get lost?
Because they know what's worth the cost!"

With every swish of clapping leaves,
The forest dances, laughs, and weaves.
Fables told by twinkling lights,
Bring together all wild sights.

So when the moonbeams softly glow,
Join the fun where the breezes flow.
The spirits laugh, each creature sways,
In the grove where humor stays.

Fern-Laden Dreams

In a patch of dreams where giggles bloom,
A hedgehog dons a tiny costume.
With branches woven in funny hats,
He parades while dodging curious cats.

The dreams are woven with silly strings,
Where every star a chuckle brings.
"Why did the snail race so slow?
He wanted to catch the moon's bright glow!"

A field of daisies laughing out loud,
Each petal joins the whimsical crowd.
With gentle breezes that tickle and tease,
Laughter bounces through leafy trees.

So drift into these fancies bright,
With each giggle, let joy take flight.
In fables spun with playful schemes,
You'll find the magic of fun-filled dreams!

www.ingramcontent.com/pod-product-compliance
Lightning Source LLC
Chambersburg PA
CBHW071833160426
43209CB00003B/280